W9-AUH-669

Tantric Massage For Beginners

Discover The Best Essential Tantric Massage- and Tantric Love Making Techniques

R. Riley

3rd Edition

FREE GIFT INSIDE

© 2015 Copyright.

Text copyright reserved. R. Riley

The contents of this book may not be reproduced, duplicated or transmitted without direct written permission from the author

Disclaimer : all attempts have been made by the author to provide factual and accurate content. No responsibility will be taken by the author for any damages caused by misuse of the content described in this book. The content of this book has been derived from various sources. Please consult a licensed professional before attempting any techniques outlined in this book.

Table of Contents

Introduction

Tantric sex is a practice that has been around for a very long time, but it's finally making its way into Western culture. It was first introduced by sex therapists who wanted to help their patients grow closer together after a long period of not being intimate, and has long since been incorporated into many bedrooms across the nation. This new method of having sex focuses on both partners' emotional, physical, and mental arousal during sex. In Western culture, physical arousal is about the only thing focused upon, which can lead to a very dry, boring experience for the female partner, and sometimes the male partner, too.

Tantric sex has been proven to help partners increase their desire for sex and their desire for one another. It is able to bring partners closer together both in the bedroom and outside of it. Mental connection between partners is just as important as emotional and physical connections during intercourse.

So if you're looking for a way to increase your enjoyment during sexual intercourse and when you're spending free time with your partner, take a look at this book to see if it can help you!

Chapter 1:
What is Tantric Sex

Tantric sex is a practice that has been happening for over 6,000 years in India. Eastern cultures adopted it due to the overwhelming amount of religions stating that sexuality was something to be rejected in order to reach enlightenment. This practice challenged the beliefs of the time and preached that sexuality was, in fact, a doorway to the divine and earthly desires such as eating, creative expression, and dancing were all sacred acts.

The word tantra translates to 'to manifest, to show, to weave, and to expand'. In the context of tantric sex, the word stands for sex expanding the consciousness and weaving together the polarities of the male and female bodies and minds into a harmonious whole.

However, couples do not have to adopt the belief system of tantric sex in order to benefit. The practice simply teaches couples to prolong their acts of making love and to utilize their orgasmic energies in a more effective manner. Tantra is also known as health enhancing.

So how is tantric sex exceptional?

Well, in Western culture, we usually view sex as recreation rather than transformation. The goal of sex is usually to pleasure ourselves rather than our partner, and we're almost never focused on connecting with our partners on a deep, emotional level. The Western culture's idea of lovemaking has a beginning and an end with a climax somewhere in between for the woman and a climax at the end for the man. It usually lasts around ten to fifteen minutes, even though a woman can take about twenty minutes to reach full arousal. For women, this type of sex can be deeply unsatisfying.

Tantric sex uses the sexual experience more like a dance where it has no beginning or an end. There isn't any specific goal, only the current moment of having sex. Sex is more like meditation and is very communicative and close. Tantra teaches a couple how to extend their sexual ecstasy peak and allows both men and women to have several orgasms in a single encounter.

Even men who experience premature ejaculation are able to extend their orgasms and even enjoy multiple orgasms with practice! And who doesn't like to practice?

To find out how you can supercharge your sex life and bring intimacy back to the bedroom, read further!

Chapter 2:
Benefits

There are many benefits to having sex, and even more benefits to having tantric sex. However, Western culture rarely sees sex as something that can be benefited from, but rather something that is no more than just a primal nuisance that humans have yet to outgrow. It is debased and degraded in modern society. But this practice has the power to bring two people together on an emotional, spiritual level and let's not forget that it has the power to bring life to this world.

So let's look at some of the benefits of this amazing, beautiful act of two people coming together.

Deeper Connection

Perhaps one of the most talked about benefits of tantric sex is that couples who explore these practices report they have lasting feelings of closeness, and they have the ability to overcome an issue better than they could before. The action of eye contact, syncing their breath, and being more aware of their partner helps them bring the relationship to an entirely different level, inside and outside of the bedroom.

Patience

Part of tantric sex is all about taking it slow. That can mean awkward movements, which most try to avoid at all costs in a dark room with their eyes closed. But by working through the confusion of tantric positions and using meditation to hold back an orgasm, the conscious connection with your partner is able to develop and you are able to develop the imperative skill of patience.

Problem-Solving

The tantric positions are usually rather difficult to figure out, especially for those who are beginners or are learning to prolong the experience without getting to an orgasm. This can require some shifting of positions and trial and error. The need to work together and talk it out in these cases in a less than modest and vulnerable position helps expand the problem-solving skills of both participants.

Creativity

When you're able to let go in one area of your life, your sex life, you're able to let go in other areas of your life, making you more creative. You're able to picture your goals more clearly because you've practiced goal-oriented sex, which is a pretty tough action on its own.

Selflessness

With tantric sex, you're able to benefit from withholding the orgasm. Tantric sex is beyond procreation and pleasure; it is about the power of liberation, an experience that is compared to getting a glimpse of the cosmic consciousness. Do not become upset if you don't reach this stage right away, especially if your partner seems to be drifting ahead of you. Supporting your out of orgasm launch into the cosmos helps you remember that giving is much better than receiving.

Empowerment

Do not confuse this with power. Empowerment is about stripping away the ego and becoming humble. It is about feeling that you do not have to hide away or be ashamed of what gives you purpose and gives you the ability to express your deepest fears and loves. There is no more hiding under the sheets, but bringing you forward into the future, instead.

Improved Sexual Health

When you perform tantric sex, you rejuvenate more than just your sex life. You are improving your sexual health. The frequent orgasms are a great way to stimulate the brain wave patterns, and alter your body's chemistry. Stress and depression will become a thing of the past, and women's sexual health and stimulation is greatly improved. It's a known fact that the more orgasms a woman has, the easier it is for her to have them. Menstrual cramps, headaches, UTI infections, incontinence, and a weak immune system are all eradicated when a woman has more orgasms.

The brain chemistry is affected by tantric sex by allowing the endocrine glands to produce more serotonin, HGH, DHEA, and testosterone. There have been scientific and medical studies that prove that sexual health will improve drastically because the blood circulation is stimulated, the body is detoxified through breath, the cardiovascular system is strengthened, the immune and endocrine systems are improved, which leads to a rejuvenated and improved sexual health, as well as overall health.

Orgasms Fortify the Immune System

Orgasms that last for twenty minutes have been proven to alleviate depression altogether. You can take years off your face when depression is eliminated from your life. You can also benefit by prolonging your lifespan, strengthening your immune system, and improving your sexual health by freeing your mind and body with tantric sex. Men have many different benefits when they participate in the act of tantric sex.

Men who are concerned with the following will benefit from this practice:

- Having erectile dysfunction

- An inability to maintain an erection

- Concerned with low intensity during sex

- Prolonging ejaculation

- Premature ejaculation

- Satisfying a partner

- Self-confidence

- Male sexual health

Male sexual health concern is more of a physical nature while women's concerns are more of a function of the mind. Women want to enjoy sex and the main problem stems from guilt or shame due to cultural beliefs about sex.

Women are concerned with the following problems during sex:

- Loss of sensation

- Loss of interest

- Painful intercourse

- Weak or mild orgasms

- Inability to reach orgasm

- Sexual shame or guilt

- Sexual health concerns

- Need to be in control

- Inhibitions

Loss of sexual interest can come from being overworked, too busy, or heaving an insensitive lover who doesn't know how to please. The shame and guilt are deeply embedded in cultural factors.

Frequent Orgasms and Women's Health

Women who have frequent orgasms benefit greatly. However, there is a big difference between having a normal climax and having a tantric climax. Ordinary orgasms are of short duration and often isolated in the sex organs like the uterus, vagina, and the clitoris. Tantric orgasms include the entire body along with the spirit and mind, and will last for hours.

Benefits of Tantric Orgasm

Tantric orgasms can only benefit greatly when it comes to health if they involve the energy and different areas of the chakras as they ascend the spinal cord. The tantric orgasm is mean to reach the central nervous system and the endocrine center, the hypothalamus and pituitary gland, on order to command the changes that will benefit sexual health.

Benefits of Frequent Orgasms

Those who have frequent and powerful orgasms will increase the levels of oxytocin their blood. Oxytocin is known as the orgasm hormone. The levels of oxytocin in your bloodstream are linked to passion, personality, emotional intelligence, social skills, and many other aspects of your behavior. This is all linked to your marriage, career, social life, and emotions. Orgasms are beneficial because they benefit the pituitary gland, which empowers brain function.

Therefore, it's safe to say that we benefit greatly from tantric sex as a species.

Chapter 3:
Importance of Sex in a Relationship

Communication is one of the most frequently used excuses for a marriage to end in divorce, yet sex and passion seem to be intimately linked with communication. Without communication, there is no sex and passion in a marriage. Without sex and passion, communication seems to be lacking in a marriage. The two are intertwined when it comes to marital sex. A good marriage is one that is defined as best friends who have passion and chemistry together. Without the passion, there isn't a marriage. Without the friends part, there isn't a marriage.

Therefore, I think it's very imperative to discuss the exact role of intimacy in a relationship and how each gender or partner has a different role, and how those roles can be nurtured and brought to life. A marriage is like a delicate kindling catching on fire. With a gentle breeze, that flame will ignite and the fire will burn long. With a strong wind, it may ignite, but it'll burn out fast and vanish. So knowing how to feed that flame of intimacy in order for it to last longer is also important.

So let's talk about gender and physiology when it comes to intimacy amongst partners.

Gender and Physiology

It's no secret that men and women are different when it comes to gender and physical appearance. It's also no secret that when it comes to intimacy, both are different. While the differences are still debated amongst scientists, psychologists, and philosophers, when it comes to sex, the differences are pretty clear cut. Unfortunately, most couples fail at reflecting on the differences and act with understanding when it comes to these differences in order to have a successful partnership.

Let's start with arousal patterns as this is the most commonly discussed difference. Men are very quick to become aroused and they are quick to orgasm, too. The spike will rise sharply and fall sharply. Men are very visual creatures, as most women know, and there is brain research to document this phenomenon. Therefore, looking at other women, videos, magazines, and pornography in general will play a large role in men's sexual life. It's one of the main reasons they love lingerie so much. Ladies, he is paying attention to what you're wearing under your clothes, and the clothes you're wearing. In fact, he's paying attention to pretty much everything you are doing if he's sexually attracted to you. So playing it up with a little sexy underwear and a hint of makeup is not shameful! It's natural for a man to be attracted to this.

Now, women take a lot longer to become aroused, but once they achieve the first orgasm, they're able to maintain that plateau of pleasure for a long time after they drop off. These two patterns between men and women are very, very different. It's not a shock, then, that it takes a lot for a couple to achieve mutual satisfaction. In fact, it almost seems like it's against nature. But the difference should not be ignored if both partners are going to be satisfied. Instead, they have to be joined in with the lovemaking process in order for both the man and the woman to find pleasure.

Regardless of who initiates the foreplay and the sex, the simplest way to obtain orgasm for both couples is for the man to focus more on pleasuring the woman in order to bring her to the first orgasm before he focuses on his own pleasure. This may seem sexist, but men thrive on feeling competent and women thrive on feeling sexy. What better way to achieve this than for the man to pay attention to the woman, and for him to feel that he's on his game when he brings her to a climax? And in order to bring a woman to orgasm, a man must understand how he can do it in the first place. Men are much simpler when it comes to bringing them to orgasm. Women have many different areas that need to be stimulated *and* they have to feel relaxed. Clitoral stimulation is the most important part of pleasing a woman. In fact, most women are not able to orgasm without clitoral stimulation either manually from themselves or a partner or from friction during intercourse.

It's also imperative to understand there is a physiological effect on the different genital anatomies. For men, intercourse is an external event. There are some evolutionary suggestions that this is because men were supposed to spread their seed to as many partners as they could in order to ensure that the species survived. It's part of what makes it easier for a man to separate sex from love. For women, having sex means that a man is literally entering her body and this makes it much more personal. It's a deeply personal act and men often forget this. It's why women complain that they need some intimacy before they have sex. Combine this need for intimacy with the difference in arousal patterns and it greatly explains why women must experience meaningful foreplay before they have sex.

Yet this need for foreplay seems to be a trap for women that become a large issue for numerous couples who seek professional help. When they are struggling, the women will insist on an emotional safety net and closeness in order to be sexual with their partner. This creates a barrier to making the marital relationship better because the lack of sex for the men is actually one of the central underlying complications in not resolving the issues at hand.

Women act like sex is a process of servicing men and often will deny being a sexual creature that needs to be serviced as much, if not more, than men. While some female readers might be scoffing at this point, consider that this statement is most of the core concepts of books written on the theme of women's sexual satisfaction in mind by many infamous, female authors.

Women must have sex for themselves! It's imperative to overcome this excuse of emotional disconnection between partners and have sex as frequently as possible and do it in a way that will build up that emotional bond at the same time. It allows both partners to feel closer with one another and creates an intimate context in which partners can then alleviate other problems in the marriage. Unless a relationship is verbally or physically abusive, both partners should make the commitment to have sex several times a week, even if they're angry! Using the tantric sex foreplay practices in this book will help drive that intimacy level up and it will help partners begin to see eye to eye again.

Women Need to Feel Desired and Men Need to Feel Competent

Another factor that comes into play when it comes to the difference in gender and sex is the physiological needs that are exercised in the sexual relationship. Women have this never-ending need and desire to feel attractive and sexy. Unfortunately, this can lead them into the trap of feeling that they must objectify themselves and minimize their own sexuality in order to focus on being the desired object of their male partners.

In reality, women who are knowledgeable about their sexuality, figuratively and literally, are the masters of their bedroom. They are in control and can shape the sexual relationship because they have a longer state of arousal. In fact, most men are secretly or openly aroused by a woman who takes a dominant role in the sexual relationship. Women have been socially conditioned to believe that they should be the chasee rather than the one chasing, and so they respond to this in a negative manner. They associate a male initiator with the one who is telling them they are desirable.

Men have the burden of being sexually competent. They are the ones who have to get an erection and keep that erection long enough to be of satisfaction to their partner. This can cause some serious performance anxiety for men. Premature ejaculation and erectile dysfunction are two of the most major complications that come with this psychological burden. The erectile dysfunction can be treated with medications while the premature ejaculation can be treated with strategies, but the key is to make it more acceptable for men to be comfortable discussing and dealing with these problems. For men who okay functionally, the most important aspect of a physical relationship is for the man to feel that he is successful. He can achieve this by making his partner aroused by being affectionate and having a reasonable amount of foreplay. The key is to bring the woman to orgasm first. If the man follows those rules, then he will have a happy partner and feel that he is a competent partner because he is.

A common problem with women, especially those who have recently had a child, is sleep deprivation. This causes a loss of libido. It's important to realize there is not a lack of need for sex, but just that women are too tired to think about it. So when the baby naps, women should be spending some quality time with their husband or alone with something that stimulates them in order to feel re-energized and relieved of stress. There is no shame in being a new mother and still being a fully functioning woman!

Differences in Libido

One of the more difficult challenges is that couples will have a naturally significant difference in their sex drive levels. Some will have a high sex drive and want to have sex all the time, or others might be happy with infrequent sexual encounters and have a low sex drive. Usually, couples are so close to the middle of this pendulum swing that they can be satisfied with that one and a half times average that people will have sex per week. But when they have a different level of need, and sometimes it may seem like there is a physiological difference while sometimes there is actually a lack of chemistry, which can create a real challenge.

Like any other issue in relationships, the solution is finding a compromise that will make a win-win situation. The answer is never going outside of the relationship, even with consent, in order to fill an unmet need because this will harm the relationship. However, masturbation is acceptable and healthy in a relationship if there is mutual consent that this is okay. Toys, videos, and touching are all forms of masturbation. The important part is making sure both partners know that there is nothing wrong with their needs and that neither one of them are doing anything wrong.

Scheduling Sex

The time issue is always something that couples will face. There never seems to be enough time in order to get together as a couple. If you want to wait for a quiet moment to have a romantic encounter that will have energy that will prolong the lovemaking, you are going to be waiting for a long time. You'll most likely only have sex a few times a year, at best. The truth is that you have to schedule a date night where you can get away from the kids, away from life, and have fun together! Make sure there is time for the two of you to still have fun by going to bed early. Neither one of you should be tired yet! Lock the door to prevent any unexpected interruptions, and don't limit yourself just to nights! Many couples find that the best time to get together is in the morning before work and after the children have left, on a lunch break when they can meet back at the house together, or even in the early afternoon before the children have come home.

If the kids are older and able to understand sex, then don't hide the fact that their parents are doing it! Sexual encounters are supposed to be expressions of love, and if children believe their parents never have sex, they then start to believe their parents are not in love. Therefore, don't hide the fact that the two of you need some alone time together and tell the kids to stay out past a certain time or stay over at a friend's house that night. Of course, they're going to make faces and make fun, but they'll be relieved to know that their parents are getting along and are in love.

And to address the issue that some people believe that sex cannot be schedule because it will not be romantic, try it one time. I guarantee you that after some gentle touching and arousal techniques described in this book later on, you will be ready to go in no time! Neither one of you will care or even think about the fact that the time was scheduled.

Research has shown that those who have sex, whether it is scheduled or not, are less likely to fight for forty-eight hours after the sexual encounter. Therefore, scheduling a sexual encounter every few days will keep both partners happy!

Communication Before, During, and After

Words are extremely erotic. You can do the same physical act repeatedly and yet it can become different every time if you use different words. Whether you talk dirty or you paint a picture of what you're going to do to your partner, expressions of desire and love will definitely help the experience along in a great way. It tells the woman, and the man, just how desirable they are to each other.

Another part of communication that is important is letting your partner know what feels good to you and what doesn't while it's happening, or ask for something that you wish to experience. That should all happen during sex! Most couples actually do this and so it's not a big problem, but what happens before and after are where the communication lines fall short. Tantric sex can help with that, but so can a lot of other things.

Couples are often embarrassed to talk with each other during general conversation to tell each other what they like and do not like. Everyone assumes that they must know how to be a good lover, but how can you do that if you don't talk about it with your partner? Of course, the other issue is talking about sex after the encounter. Most women and men are afraid to pipe up about what they liked and did not like during the encounter. They're afraid of embarrassing someone or asking for something weird and embarrassing themselves. But no one knows what the other person likes until it's discussed. So while the two of you are together and snuggled up after sex, spend a moment to rehash the parts you really loved about the whole thing. Do not use that time to be critical of the other person, though! Talking about what is not working should be done when neither one of you are aroused or in the mood for sex. It should be a casual conversation saved for a time when you're far from the sexual encounter mode.

Unfortunately, some people cannot tell a partner what they really enjoy because they actually don't know themselves, and this is a serious issue. This is where exploration and learning about different aspects of sex should be taken up by both partners in order to make the partner who isn't as knowledgeable feel comfortable with someone they trust.

Sex as Fun, a Release of Tension, and Good Exercise

We live in a world where we are constantly under pressure and feeling stressed, and we're always looking for a good way to unwind and escape from our real-life concerns. Plus, we're always looking for a way to shed some calories, too! Sex provides you with all of those benefits. One single encounter that is around forty-five minutes will help you feel calm and relaxed for forty-eight hours afterward! So turn on the lights, no more sex in the dark, and bring out the oils. Get in a good rubdown and then practice some of the exercises found later in this book.

Different Kinds of Sex

There are actually three different types of consensual sex. There is hook-up sex, marital, and making love sex. The three different kinds of sex occur on different planes, or different levels of the animal, physical, relational and spiritual beings. The conflicts and the type of sex you have are deeply embedded in the relationship you learn and how you practice this relationship with your partner.

Let's talk more about the different types of sex.

Hook-Up

Hook-up sex is using your partner for your own sexual gratification and not really caring about their needs. You both are using each other's bodies for pleasure, and while this can be intense and arousing with lust toward a new partner, it's also the most primitive and least involved type of sex. It's going after your most primitive, animal part of the human psyche. It's really just a form of playing through using each other's bodies and has nothing to do with an emotional connection. Although, it is often confused with an emotional connection, hook-up sex is purely physical.

Hook-up sex is often turned into a technique dominated sport rather than any real connection at all. In fact, many men who dominate this expertise of hook-up sex actually know about tantric methods and will abuse them in order to get the best out of the encounter.

Marital

When two people who are in a committed relationship do not have sex very often, and when they do have sex it's not as satisfying as it once was, this is known as marital sex. Marital sex is a stage that most couples will reach a few times during their relationship, but most partners still feel emotionally connected to one another and still want to make things work.

Marital sex is a higher plane than hook-up sex because there is still a degree of intimacy and emotional connection. Unfortunately, all the conflicts and the emotional battery a couple went through is then drug into the bedroom and sex becomes entangled with those emotions.

Let's say, for example, a woman is dealing with not being able to tell her husband what she wants sexually because she is dealing with some residual conflicts from her childhood where her mother called that type of woman a whore or a slut. While the woman is dealing with that in therapy, she's still having problems in the bedroom with her husband. Even learning new moves is not going to help out a couple like this.

Martial sex can actually include hook-up sex when there is an emotional high or a high brought on by legal or illegal drugs. And while this may happen in a relationship, those who experience marital sex still have some form of connection and like one another, or they had at one point in the relationship.

The good part of the relational connection is that the couples are both more humanly evolved and do have the ability to move toward the Making Love type of sex. The bad part about that is that conflicts, hurt feelings, non-mutual behavior, manipulation, and hiding out can all come into play during this stage of sexual intercourse. For example, the woman might withhold sex from the man in order to punish him for something he did, or she might use it in order to gain leverage over a partner. There might be projection or reenactment of sibling, parental, or unresolved family issues in a relationship.

In short, those who have martial sex usually bring in the external conflicts and unspoken issues into the bedroom.

Making Love

For most people, they can never evolve past martial sex due to external and internal factors in the relationship. They are never able to obtain a spiritual or emotional connection with their partner that is very deep and unbreakable. Yet, when they are able to break past that barrier between them, a couple is able to obtain a mind-body-spirit connection that is known as making love.

Tantric sex is one of the ways to obtain making love, but this ego-less state can only be attained if both partners are open with one another and feel that they are equal. They can only obtain this level of intimacy through communication and behavior that speaks of equality rather than bringing bad vibes into the bedroom. That is why you will need to focus on the beginning exercises and be completely comfortable and sure that you are ready to move past them before you do.

The physical part of making love is aimed at increasing, building, and exchanging a sexual energy of your partner's body. They are both important pathways to steadily expanding and elevating pleasure throughout the entire body. In contrast to balloon sex, which is when two partners get together for hook-up sex, this form deepens, broaden, sustains, and expands arousal and positive tension between partners. Orgasm is no longer the end result that both partners rush for. Making love is not about genital intercourse at all. Those who are unable or do not have genital sex are still able to get to the heightened, mind-body-spiritual state of mind of Making Love.

Most of the sexual techniques used to get to making love have a common belief system of breathing meditative and physical movement techniques with your partner. Combined with a longer foreplay, this will leave to the status of making love or tantric sex. They help you forget about your ego needs like wanting to receive pleasure or wanting to give pleasure.

While these sexual techniques help you increase and build energy give-and-take and flow, the quality and amount of arousal and pleasure you and your partner will experience sexually will depend on the degree to which you two are building a connection and arousal in other parts of the relationship.

You can obtain these other areas through mutual respect and understanding, and being transparent about your emotions and inner thoughts. You feel more excited and stimulated then, and you feel connected as equals.

Chapter 4:
Types of Intimacy

Intimacy is not a thing, it is a process. It will take some time to develop intimacy and is not something that stagnates. The stagnation in the relationship is what *kills* intimacy. Intimacy can come in many different forms.

Cognitive

Cognitive intimacy is where a couple will exchange their ideas, thoughts, and enjoy each other's similarities and differences between opinions. If they are able to do this in an open and comfortable way, then they can become very intimate in the intellectual area.

Experiential

Experiential intimacy is when a couple is involved in an activity together that most likely doesn't involve a lot of talking. They get together actively and involve themselves with each other, and keep their thoughts or feelings to themselves, but they're involved in a mutual activity together. Imagine that a couple is painting a fence and the brush strokes are in unison. The two people painting are involved in an experiential intimacy.

Emotional

This is the form that most women think about when they think about intimacy. It's the form where two people are able to share their feelings and thoughts comfortably with one another. They can empathize with the emotions of the other person, and really understand and be aware of the other person's emotions.

Sexual

This is the type of intimacy that most people think about when they hear the word intimacy. This form actually includes a large range of sensuous activities and is more than just intercourse. It's any form of sensual expression with one another. Therefore, intimacy can be a very different thing from person to person, depending on the situation.

Blockades

Of course, just like anything, there are some complications that can crop up when it comes to intimacy. Some of these complications may include:

- Communication. This is a barrier where one person enters into a relationship and some a mistaken or preconceived notion of what intimacy is and misjudges the needs or thoughts of the other person. Communication or lack of communication can be one of the main barriers that form when trying to create a foundation of intimacy in a relationship.

- Time. Intimacy is going to take some time to develop and a person who isn't willing to allow the proper amount of time for intimacy to develop is not going to be able to develop that type of relationship.

- Awareness. It's necessary for a person to know of themselves, and to know of their partner, too. Those who are not aware of their personal tastes and intimacy are not able to be aware of another person. At least not in the terms of actual intimacy with the other person.

- Shyness. The reluctance to share your thoughts and emotions with another person can also keep intimacy from developing in a relationship. You have to be open to what you're thinking and feeling in order for someone else to know them.

- Game Playing. Those who try to fit into a stereotypical role or play a certain type of game, even if they are intimacy appearing games, like a romantic game, can't develop the intimate relationship they need with someone else because they are not themselves. Game playing is a disadvantage to the development of intimacy.

Developing Intimacy

Developing intimacy takes two different ingredients, awareness, and knowledge.

- Awareness. This is being aware of who you are and where you are, and not trying to start in another place. Start with the form of intimacy that you're comfortable with and if a particular form is difficult to you, then that's not the place for you to begin to develop intimacy with another person. If you're comfortable with intellectual intimacy, then share thoughts and talk with that person about their ideas and opinions. Once you're more comfortable in that area, that start to develop the other areas.

- Knowledge. Not every intimate relationship has to include all the different aspects of intimacy itself. There are many compatible and satisfied couples out there who are in an intimate relationship using only emotional and intellectual intimacy.

Chapter 5:
Beginning Exercises

When you first begin tantra, you may not experience an orgasm for a few weeks. That's because these following exercises are all about reconnecting with your partner rather than actually performing the act of sex. These steps are meant to teach you that intercourse is not the ultimate goal and that giving and receiving pleasure using gentle touches and loving words is the goal.

As you're performing these exercises, communicate with your lover to figure out what they find most arousing. For many couples, performing these exercises help lovers forget about the pressure of going all the way and allows them to release sexual guilt, build up trust and reawaken their sexual desires.

Welcome Love

The first step to this exercise is to make time for each other every week. Plan a time where the two of you will be intimate at least once a week and set aside an hour or more of uninterrupted time to just be together. Your relationship has to be a priority, so if you have to find someone to babysit children, then find that person.

The second step is to create an inviting atmosphere. You don't have to meet in your bedroom. You could meet up in the living room, kitchen or even the bathroom for a tub date! Just be sure to light some candles, lay out some fresh flowers, find some finger foods to enjoy together, enjoy a few pieces of erotic art, and light some incense for an erotic aroma. You don't have to go all out though. You could just dim the light and play a little erotic music in order to create a welcoming environment.

The third step is to dress daringly, or wear nothing! You should experiment with clothing and accessories that make you feel erotic, as well as turn your partner on.

Intimacy Exercises

When you first start out with the intimacy exercises, you want to start with a ritual. This can something as simple as sitting and gazing into each other's eyes or feeding each other finger foods. You can even share a glass of wine nude, or bathe together in order to be in tune with each other.

Take the time to wash each other, feed each other, and listen to each other speak as you talk about your day or talk about things you enjoy. Even if it's something you may have talked about before, we oftentimes forget what our partners enjoy in life and need a good refresher.

Next, massage each other or read to each other. Dance and play music or sing together. Do something together that makes you fuse your energies and develop some new intimacy skills. Use the time you have together in order to communicate and share what you like about each other. You're aiming to help your partner feel loved and cherished, and understood, above all else.

This is where it gets tricky. Some will choose to perform these rituals for only a week while others may choose to perform this ritual for a few months before they actually hit the sack together. This is a personal choice and this step should never be rushed! After all, if you're a couple who has been at rock bottom for a few years, it could take up to six months before the two of you feel you can trust each other again. Intimacy takes time, and when it's a matter of the heart, it shouldn't be rushed.

Deep Breathing Exercise

Breathing is something we usually don't think about doing unless we're having some serious trouble doing it, so when you consciously breathe, you become much more aware of your surroundings and who you're with. So try this exercise with your partner.

Sit quietly with your legs crossed and face each other. Place your hand son your knees with your palms facing up and gaze into your partner's eyes. Take very soft, deep breaths as you each gaze at one another, and then try to gaze beyond the eyes but into the soul. This may feel very awkward and you both may find yourselves smiling as you do this, but just keep your gazes fixed and refrain from speaking. Eye contact is essential for intimacy to be built up.

Pay special attention to your breathing as you perform this exercise. Breathe at the same pace as your partner, bringing air slowly in through the nose and exhaling through the mouth. Remember to maintain eye contact as the two of you breathe together. Practice until the two of you can keep eye contact and breathe at the same time for a total of ten minutes. Then move to the next exercise.

Erotic Touch

This experiment takes place as you're both practicing the eye contact exercise, but synchronized breathing is not as essential to this step. Your breath will come back into the picture later on. Guide your partner as you take turns stimulating each other and describe how you want to be touched.

Share your desires in a positive manner and make requests in a clear but loving manner. Ask your lover to caress an erogenous zone and encourage them to apply more or less pressure. Let them know if you want them to use a specific pattern or if you want them to use their tongue or another part of their body. Thank them and allow them to know that you are enjoying their sensual touches.

When the two of you are comfortable with this, you may want to create a pleasure chest. Add toys that excite you and your partner such as a feather, some massage oil, a vibrator, some soft fabric, a blindfold, or maybe some erotic notes or cards. As you pleasure each other, do not ever feel ashamed to ask for something different. This is a time for experimentation, appreciation, and taking responsibility for your own fulfillment rather than letting your partner stumble around in the dark.

From this exercise, you should take it to the next level and create adventures together. Explore the new and creative ways you can awaken each other. Then, and only then, will you be able to enjoy and practice tantric lovemaking properly.

Chapter 6:
Basic Tantric Sex Techniques

There are some basic techniques you need to learn before you dive right into the different positions. You can use these techniques in order to heighten the arousal and pleasure you obtain from the positions described in the final chapter of this book.

The tantric tradition emphasizes the preparation for lovemaking or foreplay. The erotic rituals described in the previous chapter where two couples exchange pleasures helps the individuals awaken their senses and allows them to communicate on emotional and physical levels.

Lovers can establish and maintain an intimate connection as they transition into sex. These intimacy workouts are a form of prolonged foreplay and help stimulate lovers for the sexual experience they're about to have. These are the ideal conditions for tantric lovemaking.

When you are experimenting with these techniques, don't worry if you're doing something the right or wrong way. It's not about that. It's about your pleasure and your partner's pleasure, and the two of you will know what feels and is right.

As you move into the act of sex, the idea of tantric sex is to maintain that state of sexual ecstasy for as long as the two of you can. It's not about results, but about a timeless and unstructured event.

Maintain Intimacy

As the two of you are engaging in sexual intercourse, be sure to maintain eye contact if the position allows for it. Wherever you can, sprinkle kisses on your lover's flesh and whisper words of love and encouragement to them. Help them feel that you love and desire them.

Be Slow

In Western culture, sexual intercourse is focused upon instant gratification and oftentimes leaves the woman feeling dissatisfied. Tantric sex is about keeping the sexual encounter slow and purposeful. This allows men to control when they orgasm and allows women to get to the peak of their sexual arousal. During this time of going slow, focus on each other and if your thoughts wander, bring them back to what you're currently doing. Concentrate on your lover and the magic of the moment rather than anything else.

Bring Attention to Breathing

Breathing is very important for men and women. You ought to resist the urge to breathe quickly as this creates arousal and speeds your path to orgasm. Instead, take long and slow breaths from the belly and exhale gradually. Try to match your breath to your partner or breathe alternately. When you inhale, you partner exhales during gradual breathing. This will move the energy back and forth and connect you with your lover in a deeper manner.

Vary Positions

Another thing lacking from Western culture is varied positions. Different positions will add to sexual pleasure and balance the male and female energies. When you release yourself from a gender role, such as man on top and woman on the bottom, then you are able to have deeper, more intimate sex. Sometimes men want to feel soft and vulnerable during sex and feel that their partner is gentle. Women will often enjoy being able to direct and initiate. When you experiment with different positions, the woman dominate and the man submissive or vice versa, explore your ability to be a strong or gentle lover.

Multiple Orgasms for Men

Did you know that men can have an orgasm without actually ejaculating? They often will ejaculate with their orgasm, but they can have multiple orgasms without ejaculating until the end of a sexual encounter. Ejaculation control is the epitome of Tantric lovers capturing and extending their magical energies of orgasm. When men hold back ejaculation, they can experience mini-orgasms.

This essence of this is to find the wave and surf it almost to the top but to never go over the edge. You can use some of these strategies of you're a man.

PC Muscles

The pub coccygeal muscles run from your pubic bone to your tailbone and are the ultimate sex muscles. They are the same muscles that control the flow of urine. If properly trained, the muscles enable a man to stop ejaculation as they continue to enjoy sex. Kegel exercises are not only for women, but also for men.

Men can exercise their PC muscles by contracting them three times a day, squeezing twenty to twenty-five times each time they practice. This is something that a man can do any time, but it should not be overdone. After a month of practicing, try extending the squeeze and hold each contraction for two seconds. Gradually work up to ten seconds. When they're in good shape, men are able to ride the orgasmic wave without going over the top.

Relax

It may seem paradoxical to say, but it's imperative that men are able to relax during a high state of arousal. If a man feels that he's going to ejaculate, then he should take a few steadying breaths and stop having intercourse just long enough for the arousal to subside. Then he can relax and try again.

Experimenting this way will allow a man to know how much time he needs in between mini orgasms in order to keep from ejaculating. The idea is to allow the man enough time for the intensity to subside, but not so much so that he loses his erection.

Put It Together

First, don't expect this to work the first time. There are going to be 'wipe-outs' or 'accidents', so don't rely on this as a good 'pull-out' method. Protection should always be used in order to prevent pregnancy if pregnancy is not the end goal.

As the man is making love to his partner, he should thrust slowly and allow his arousal to build gradually. Before his excitement gets too far, he should relax a moment and tighten his PC muscles as he takes a deep breath. Resume making love and continue to generate excitement.

Then, relax again and hold the PC's as you breathe. Continue to ride the wave until you are almost near the crest, and then open your eyes and clamp down on 9our PC muscles and take a deep breath.

Multiple Orgasms for Women

Women's most powerful organ for sex lies between their ears and not between their legs. Desire is often circumvented by fear, stress, guilt, and other distracting thoughts for women. Women must concentrate on feeling rather than thinking as they're having sex, and taking breaks to pleasure one another helps them ward off lingering diversions and coax more orgasms.

Clitoral Stimulation

A majority of women actually require that the clitoris and labia are stimulated in order to achieve orgasm. The labia is the inner lips that surround the clitoris. Prolonged, gentle stroking is usually the key for sexual ecstasy. For women, they need to show their partner how to stroke them in order to achieve orgasm. Be gentle and positive because for men it's very difficult to get the rhythm just right. But when they do, you'll be glad!

G-Spot Stimulation

In the tantric belief system, the g-spot is known as the sacred spot. It's a powerful and enigmatic erogenous zone located about two or three inches up on the front side of the vaginal canal. When the woman is aroused, she should have her lover slip his ring finger into the vagina and stroke up with his fingertip to brush against the inner wall.

The g-spot is around the size of a pea or up to the size of a quarter and has a somewhat rippled texture. For some women, a gentle stimulation can induce a powerful orgasm that may lead to female ejaculation. Over stimulating this sensitive spot can lead to discomfort, so be careful!

Lovers who practice these ancient techniques are able to channel sexual energy through the chakras or energy centers. They can move the energy of an orgasm through these physical channels and create sensations of sexual ecstasy through their body that actually enhance their health.

Now that you know about the different techniques and the practices let's take a look at tantric massage as foreplay.

Chapter 7:
Tantric Massage Introduction

Tantric massage can be performed by both men and women, and should be a part of sexual foreplay in order to get both partners warmed up and ready for intercourse. Some of these techniques may not be comfortable for you or your partner, so just go with what feels right and don't rush or push anything.

Just as there is a misunderstanding of the world Tantra, there are many misunderstandings of the words Tantra massage. In many people's minds, this brings about the thoughts of a massage that has a happy ending, or a sexual release, and there are many out there who are performing Tantra massage and doing just that. However, massage in Tantra is much more profound and deeper than just a sexual release.

Massages given for sexual pleasure should be termed erotic massage, but what is Tantra massage then?

Tantra is a life path of spiritual awakening. There are hundreds of different methods of awakening described in the ancient texts, such as meditating, eating mindfully, and meditative sexual union. This ancient text also includes the meditation of touch.

Tantra is a union of opposites, meaning the meeting of yin and yang. Therefore, it invites the polarities or the opposites to come together. Tantra massage may come in bodily form, but it's much more than just sex. It is sharing the energies of yin and yang.

One of the ways that Tantra massage is different from a normal massage is that it invites *both* forms of energy into the massage. Yin is the energy of relaxation, and that's the form of energy most experience when they're getting a massage at a spa. However, Tantra massage invites yang to also join in, which is the stimulating energy. Tantra massage done right is meant to build up and break down energy throughout the process. This is meant to bring about a sense of peace to both parties, the one giving and the one receiving.

Because this type of massage works with energy, it's possible to give a Tantra massage without massaging the sex organs. Yin and yang can be stimulated through the spine and the energy of the body. There are many who achieve a full body orgasmic experience while their clothes are still on, but be aware that an orgasmic state is not an essential part of this massage technique.

Tantra massage brings about the union of sexual organs with the other parts of the body, which is a union of sexual energy with the other life forces that are flowing through a person. Even if the receiver doesn't have an orgasmic experience during the massage, they often find that it makes a difference in the way the energy flows through them the next time they're in a sexual act. Many couples receive great benefits through this healing method.

Sexual organ massage also releases some past sexual traumas, especially when they're given by a therapist who's well trained. It's important to create a safe space when Tantra massage is going to happen. This helps support the receiver's process of healing.

There are a few different ways that you can receive a Tantra massage. The first way is to seek out a therapist who understands the boundaries of not participating in the orgasmic experience. The second is to ask a lover to perform one if they know how. And the third is going to a workshop with a lover in order to learn how to perform and receive a Tantra massage.

So now that you know the basics of a Tantra massage, let's talk more about how to perform one.

Chapter 8:
Performing Tantric Massage

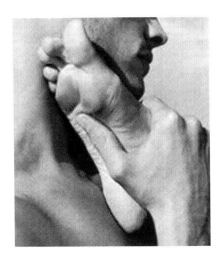

Before we get into the details of a tantric massage, there should first be a discussion of the benefits and the boundaries for tantric massage.

Benefits

When it comes to tantric massage, there are many different benefits, and not all of them are related to sexual arousal. Let's take a look at them in this section and you can determine if the benefits are something for you.

Improve Breathing

Tantric massage is often combined with pranayama, a breathing technique used during meditation. It's intended to move energy through the body in a more effective manner. When it's regularly performed, Tantra massage and the breathing techniques used with it improve your overall breathing techniques. This is able to improve alertness and exercising abilities. Improving breathing and relaxation are also able to improve healing from injury and disease.

Body and Mind Relaxation

Like other types of massage, tantric massage is able to be used to relax the body. In addition to physical ailments being released, tantric massage can also release emotional pain. Many claim that they feel less fearful or guilty after they receive a tantric massage. Some will find that they feel more energized and alert, which lets them become more active during the day and sleep better at night.

Sexual Arousal

A section about the benefits of tantric massage wouldn't be complete without a section on sexual arousal. Tantra massage is a great way to create sexual arousal between two people. When it's performed between lovers, tantric massage strengthens the connection between the couple and leads to a more intimate evening. However, given that this is a potential effect of massage, it's imperative to remember that this can also happen with a professional. In a professional setting, it's important that you inform the giver if they are going beyond comfortable boundaries. Let them know you're feeling these sensations and let them know if you are uncomfortable.

Now that you're aware of the benefits of tantric massage let's take a look at some guides on how to get started.

Boundaries

When it comes to performing a tantric massage, there should be boundaries discussed by the giver and receiver. Here are some common ones laid out between a giver and receiver who do not know one another well.

- No touching of the genitals.

- No kissing, cuddling, or holding.

- No toys.

Of course, those boundaries do not have to apply if you are comfortable with them and if the giver is also comfortable with them. If Tantra massage is being performed by a couple who have known each other a while, then those boundaries most likely won't apply.

The important thing is to be communicative and upfront about what you want in the massage if you are the receiver, and what you are comfortable with if you are the giver.

Beginning Tantra Massage

When you first start out with tantric massage, it's important to know some of the details before you start practicing. This is an outline of what might happen during a tantric massage, whether you're the giver or receiver.

Comfortable Atmosphere

A comfortable atmosphere is the first step to a tantric massage. There should be some gentle lighting like candles in order to minimize any distractions. If there are not candles at your disposal, you can also lower the wattage of the lamps in order to dim the light. Choose some soft music to play or light a few incense to create an intimate and relaxed atmosphere.

Lie Facedown

Now that the stage has been set, the person who is receiving the massage is going to lie face down on the surface that's been provided. They should lie with their arms in a 'v' shape away from the body, and their legs should be spread in a 'v' shape, too. The giver might choose to position the limbs themselves in order to create an intimate connection from the start. Then the receiver and giver will both focus on their breathing, focusing on keeping their breaths in sync as the massage begins.

Personalized

From that moment on, the massage is going to be personalized and dependent on the connection the giver has with the receiver. Hands will be moved over the person's body, starting with a few light fingertip strokes and moving on to a whole hand stroke and some caresses. There shouldn't be restrictions on where the hands are able to explore and not explore. They should be applied evenly over the body for the duration of the massage. Performing in this way will make both the giver and receiver comfortable.

Mutual Relation

When a tantric massage is given, it's imperative that the giver and receiver focus on the connection between them. The energy is going to promote a healthy intimacy and relaxation between the couple. If there is a strong connection with your partner when there's a massaging of a certain spot, then focus on that spot for a longer period of time. Pay attention to how the receiver reacts to the amount of pressure being used so that the giver can feel relaxation.

Sexual Performance

It's important to note that Tantra massage is not really about sexual practice. It's about focusing on creating a sensual mood between two people and aligning the energies of their bodies. The massage is supposed to be peaceful and relaxing rather than completely stimulating. Massaging the sexual organs is not necessary unless both people are comfortable with that type of connection. It can start out as a more casual massage and move into a sensual method of massage if there is an intimate connection.

So how can a woman please a man during a tantric massage if she wants to take things further as the giver? Read the next chapter to find out!

How to Set the Mood

When it comes to sensual massages and tantric massage, setting the mood is one of the most important things. The massage is meant to be sensual, and your partner needs to feel as comfortable as they can be.

First, you want to dim the lights and light a few candles. This provides you and your partner with a romantic ambiance to work with. Next, prepare the massage area. Find a firm surface for your partner to lie down on and put down a towel in case there's oil involved. If you're just giving someone a scalp massage, a chair will do, too.

Second, you want to play some music. You don't want something like AC/DC to be playing, choose something soft and soothing like Liquid Mind. Be sure you know what the goal is here. It's either to make your partner relaxed, ready for sex, or put them to sleep. If a massage is supposed to be an appetizer for the main course, choose something sexy to play like soul music. If it's for relaxation, then try some slow and soft blues. If it's to put someone to sleep, running water and rainforest sounds are good. Bottom line, the music is going to set the mood for the entire massage, so choose wisely.

The oil is the main ingredient to the massage. It's as important as a wrench is to a mechanic. There are many oils you can use for massage, such as jojoba, hemp, apricot kernel, hazelnut, avocado, argan, rosehip seed, safflower, camellia, walnut, macadamia nut, coconut, almond, marula, grapeseed, Moringa, sesame, sunflower, borage, and mustard oil are all excellent choices. You should experiment with some of them and maybe mix a few together to get the right texture and scent you're looking for.

You can find all of those oils and many more at your local health food store. In addition, skincare stores and spa shops also have a large variety of massage oils that are already blended. These are also very appealing, and the store clerk can help you figure out which one might be right for the night you're trying to set up.

Almond oil is a favorite for many because it's a little oily, which allows the hands to glide smoothly. Also, it doesn't get absorbed too easily, so it doesn't have to be constantly reapplied.

Warm up the Traps

Tension and tightness in this muscle located between the shoulder blades is a common complication for those who carry around a lot of stress throughout the day. Loosen up your partner's trap muscles by putting a little massage oil or lotion at the base of the spine. Cross your thumbs together and slip them up the spine to the point between the shoulder blades. Then use the thumbs to massage the upper back and release tension stored there.

Tapping

Gently tap the small of your partner's back with the edges of your hands. This actually stimulates an erotic zone and the nerve impulses go directly to the genitals.

Use Lips

This is an excellent way to be close to your partner and really feel intimate. Instead of using your hands, wipe off any excess oil or lotion and take a deep breath. Then run your lips from the base of your partner's spine to the nape of their neck. Keep one lip on either side of their spine so that your lips are straddling your partner's backbone. Exhale slowly as you move your lips up your partner's back. The warm breath will ignite their nerves.

Make Friction

Use your hands to work your way up your partner's back from the base of their spine to the nape of their neck. Make sure to go slowly and use your dominant hand. Repeat this motion gently with an up and down motion with the heel of your hand. Only go a few inches at a time and use the dry friction in order to generate heat.

Make it Hot

Repeat the friction rub from the last step but do it between your partner's shoulder blades. This will heat up their muscles and help them relax.

Warm up a Man's Genitals

Straddle your partner and face their feet. Start at the ankle and use your thumb and forefinger in order to apply pressure on either side of the tendon and you work your way up the leg. Don't apply pressure to the actual tendon, though. There's a pressure point along the tendon that stimulate the prostate in men and connects to their genitals. The man will notice a tingling in his leg that will eventually move to his genital area.

Full Body Massage

If you're not already nude, then take off your clothes and lay down a towel on the bed. Have your partner lie down on the bed and then slather up the front of your body with some lotion or massage oil. Then move your body across your partner's back and front, but don't allow penetration.

Stimulate the Man's Nipples

This is a highly erogenous zone in men that is almost always neglected by women. As the woman is lying on top of the man, have her use her mouth to lick and suck at the man's nipples. This will most likely feel very good to him. However, there are some men who report that nipple stimulation is actually a turn-off, so be careful about what he does and does not like.

So now you have all the ingredients and the idea of what tantric massage is, so it's time to learn a few different techniques. The part of the body the man is going to massage depends on his relationship with her, and vice versa. If you've been a couple for a while, a full body tantric massage will definitely be a hit. However, if the two of you are just getting to know each other, then try out a few techniques on the hands instead.

Shiatsu

This is the main technique that's used in Japan and is relatively easy to learn. If you've had a nice back massage before where someone rubbed out the knots in your muscles with their thumbs, then you've had a shiatsu massage.

Simply lay your hands or fingers on a spot while applying a little pressure and rotate slowly. Your hands should be oiled at this point to avoid painful friction. Try to find a few knots on your partner's back and gently massage them away. If you're comfortable and they're not in pain, you can use your elbow to gently apply more pressure to some areas to get out the knots.

Compression

This is another common technique used in most massage forms. Just press down on one area and increase blood flow while loosening the muscles. This is a good technique to do before doing something deeper like shiatsu. It's a great warmup technique that will get the body singing. It's also a great technique for the butt, where one hand can be placed on top of the other and rotated slowly.

Stroking

Stroking is just long, gentle movements using your hands along your partner's body. Keep the fingers together and the thumb parallel. The palms should be in contact with the body. This technique is very pleasing on all areas of the body.

Friction

This is an advanced technique that is used on people's hands and feet. The friction technique does not work well with the use of oils, so wipe off your hands if you were using any. This is a focused stroke used in a small area of the body with a little stability and pressure. Good places for beginners to try this move are the hands and feet. Otherwise, if you're partner's careful, you can try it on their genital area.

Kneading

Kneading is a good way to get deep into the muscles and is a good technique to use on the most fleshy areas of the body, such as the behind. If you're doing it gentle, you can do it anywhere, but do not do this on the woman's stomach if hers isn't flat. She might feel uncomfortable.

Kneading is a lot like kneading a loaf of bread. If you've never made bread before, it's actually pretty easy. The way you do it is by grasping and a little bit of the tissue and lifting it, but no too high. First the palms will press down on the muscle tissue; you will gently push your fingers together, and then move upward in a lifting motion.

All of the aforementioned massages go very well together. You can apply some shiatsu to your partner's shoulder with a little oil, then stroke the back, knead the behind, stroke the calves and thighs and finish off with some friction on the soles of your partner's feet.

Full Body Rubdown

What if you want to do a full body rubdown but you're not sure how to begin? Then read this section. You'll find a step-by-step guide on how to give a full-body rubdown to your partner. The full body rubdown is used more for a sensual massage than just between friends, so be sure your partner is willing.

Head

There will no oil necessary in this part of the rubdown.

Head massages can be extremely relaxing, and they're great for those who have not really been intimate with. It's also good for women and men who are not comfortable with having sensitive areas touched just yet.

Have the receiver lie down on his or her stomach with their head on a pillow. If they are not comfortable without a massage table, they can turn their head from one side to the other from time to time. In addition, if it's easier for the giver, they can give a head massage in a chair instead.

Begin by rubbing the temples and forehead. The giver then runs their fingers through the man or woman's hair and applies some gentle, downward pressure. Massage the entire scalp in this manner for as long as the giver is comfortable, and then kiss the ears at the end if it's welcomed.

Shoulder, Back and Neck Massage

This is what people think about when they first hear the word massage, and there's a good reason for that. This is one of the most relaxing massages that someone can use on another person. It also turns a normal evening into a sensual evening.

For this massage, the receiver has to lie down on their stomach and their back has to be bare. Place a quarter sized amount of oil in the palm of your hand and warm it up by rubbing the hands together. Then begin with long strokes up the back, and then down the back. Begin to do the shiatsu massage and knead the shoulders gently. Progressively move up toward the neck.

Buttocks Massage

The buttock is a highly erotic zone that is going to crave touch. Therefore, this is a sensual massage that's excellent for romantic foreplay. Just be sure your partner is up for this. If not, move on to another area.

The giver should place their palms on the receiver's behind and massage in circular motions. Increase the pressure while gradually covering all the areas of the behind. Then the giver will place their hands on the right behind cheek and use the kneading technique. Create a roll of skin using the thumbs and push it up, but not too hard. Repeat this on the left side.

Leg Massage

For this massage, the receiver will be lying on their back. The giver will then gently stroke the thighs and calves of the receiver using a light touch with the fingertips. Be sure not to put too much pressure on the knees or kneecaps in order to avoid injury. For a leg massage, it's best to use the gentle finger swirl technique.

Foot Massage

The feet are actually a very special part of the body. They are like a sensual map that reflects the different organs and will even change a person's personality. Have the receiver lie down on their back. Don't press too much into small areas of the feet because this can lead to intestinal upset. Start at the heel and work the way up. Press gently with the thumbs and be sure not to be too soft or hard.

Hand Massage

A hand massage is a lot like a foot massage because the hands are also maps of the body. Begin up by the wrist and work your way up the hands. Massage the different areas of the hand with the thumbs and finish by gently playing with the receiver's fingertips.

Chest Massage

The chest massage is an excellent place to end a full body rubdown, but it should only be done if the partners are both comfortable. If the receiver is a woman, the giver should begin on the outside of the breasts with a gently tickling of the fingertips across the flesh. Move in a circular motion and keep eye contact with the receiver to be sure they're enjoying what is happening.

If the receiver asks for more pressure, gently and slowly apply it. By the end of the massage, the giver should be at the nipples and may also massage those, too. The giver can also squeeze the breasts together gently and rub the nipples in a circular motion, which can heighten the sense of arousal.

For men being the receiver, the woman should also perform a gentle, circular motion with the fingertips on the outside of the man's pecks. Then gently swirl inward until the receiver is aroused.

So for the full body massage, the giver should behind with the head, move on to the neck, back, and shoulder region, following through the steps outlined in this section, and end with the breast massage if the receiver is comfortable. At this point, the couple can choose to end the massage or take it further.

Tantric Breast Massage

The tantric breast massage is a little more in-depth than the chest massage mentioned in the previous section. This is a ritual that will allow the woman to receive sexual energy and love from her partner. The breast massage will focus solely on the woman's breast. Not only does this make them firmer, but it also makes them healthier and helps the woman maintain a balance of hormones in her body. Breast massage is also an excellent way for a man to give healing, pleasure, and intimacy to his partner. The breasts are the seat of the woman's sexuality, and they need to be loved and honored before any other parts of the body will open up.

Breast massage is tricky because the tissue of the breasts is delicate. However, if it's done right with only a moderate amount of pressure exerted, massaging the breasts is safe. The procedure is also very simple.

The space where the massage is going to take place should be inviting, warm, and special so that the receiver will feel comfortable and welcome. Before the giver begins, he or she should explain to the receiver that the massage is for the breasts and nothing else, and nothing else should be thought of other than receiving. It's up to the giver to make it firm that the receiver should not wonder about having to give pleasure afterward.

The breast massage should be begun with one hand on the woman's heart chakra and the other on her yoni, or the Venus mound, and visualization of the warm energy moving from the heart and into the hands down to the yoni should commence. This is a healing and connecting visualization that's used before the breast massage is begun.

In order to avoid any discomfort or friction, massage oil should be used on the skin. The application of the oil on the breasts is the first part of the massage. It should be applied in a circular movement on the breast, with the direction beginning at the center of the chest toward the underarm. Caress the breasts slowly and gently. Brush the palms of the hands over the entire breast for a smooth sensation.

Think about only the rhythm and giving. Repeat the movements several times in order to be consistent. If working in a clockwise motion, do that motion on both breasts. Or try this. Place the palm over the entire breast with the nipple at the center of the palm. Fan out the fingers as if they are the spokes of a wheel and bring them in toward the nipple. Finish with a gentle pinch and repeat.

The next step to the massage of the breasts is done when the breasts are fully covered in oil. The breast is then kneaded by lifting it from the chest and pressing carefully with both hands. This should be done in a very gentle manner. Alternate with both hands holding the breast, and twist and wrung the flesh very carefully.

The third step is to scoop the flesh of the breast with gentleness using the flat of the fingertips. The strokes need to be done clockwise, and then counterclockwise.

The fourth step is to begin massaging the nipples directly. Take your thumbs and put them on the opposite side of the nipple, beginning on the outside edge of the areola. Gently and slowly bring the thumbs together and lightly squeeze the nipple between the thumbs, pulling outward toward you. Repeat until you have made a complete circle around the nipple. Be sure to adjust pressure depending on how the receiver reacts. Some will like it light while some will like it a little harder.

The fifth step, or the final step, is to stroke the skin of the breasts with the direction of the fingertips moving from the center outward toward the side. This is a cooling down phase of the massage. When it's done, repeat all the steps on the other breast.

End this massage the same way it began by putting one hand on the heart and the other on the yoni. Visualize warm energy going from the heart into your hands and down into the yoni. Breathe deeply and slowly together for a few moments. Then allow the receiver to rest.

Breast massage can be as enjoyable for the giver as it is for the receiver. It's healing emotionally and physically for both. This is a great way to relax and perform sexual foreplay with your partner. It can be done alone or it can be combined with other tantric massages, like the g-spot massage, the yoni massage, or the clitoral massage.

Yoni Massage

Yoni is the Sanskrit word for vagina so this massage will focus on a woman's vagina only.

The receiver should lie down on her back with some pillows under her head so that she can look down at her genital area and up at the partner or giver. Another pillow, covered with a towel, should be put under her hips. Her legs must be apart with her knees somewhat bent. Place a few pillows or cushions under the knees to support her. Her genitals should be clearly displayed for the massage.

This position will allow full access to the vagina and other parts of the body. Before the giver touches the body, the massage should be begun with relaxing, deep breaths. Both the giver and receiver should breathe deeply and slowly during the process in order to remain relaxed. The giver should gently remind the receiver to breathe again if they begin to stop breathing, or if they take shallower breaths. It's imperative that the receiver not begin to hyperventilate. If that occurs, gently stop the massage and wait for the receiver to get their breathing under control.

To begin, gently massage the abdomen, legs, breasts, thighs, and arms in order to encourage the receiver to feel relaxed, and for them to prepare for the yoni to be massaged. Pour a small bit of oil or lubricant onto the mound of the yoni. Pour just enough that it drips to the outer lips and covers the outside of the yoni. Begin massaging the mound and outer labia of the yoni, spending time there and not rushing. Relax and enjoy the sensation of giving the massage.

Now, softly squeeze the external labia between your thumb and index finger, and glide up and down the whole span of the labia. Do the same for the other labia. The giver should take their time, and it's also helpful if the receiver and giver are looking into each other's eyes as much as possible. The receiver must tell the giver if the pressure, depth, or speed has to be increased or decreased. Limit the conversation and focus only on the sensation as too much talking is going to diminish the effect.

The Crown Jewel Massage

The crown jewel is also known as the glans of the clitoris, and this is a very complex, amazing structure that's similar to the tip of a man's penis, but it's actually four times more sensitive. The glans of the clitoris hold six thousand to eight thousand nerve endings, more than any other structure that's in the human body. This node has only one function, and that's pleasure. Nothing exceeds the ability to receive and transmit pressure, touch or vibration like the clitoris. The glans is known as the crown jewel or the clitoral system.

The yoni massage should be performed before the crown jewel massage because the woman is not going to enjoy it if she's not already aroused and relaxed. If the crown jewel massage is attempted before the yoni massage, the woman may feel pain and it will not be enjoyable for her.

To begin, stroke the clitoris in a clockwise and counter-clockwise movement. Lightly squeeze the clitoris between the thumb and index finger, but only as a massage and not as a way to bring the receiver to orgasm. The receiver is going to become very aroused, but encourage her to relax and breathe deeply in order to prolong the pleasure.

With care and slow speed, gently insert the middle finger of the right hand into the vagina. It should always be the right hand because the left hand will insert bad energy into her. Gently explore the inside of the vagina with this finger and massage the inside. Be gentle, take your time, feel sideways, up, and down. Vary the speed, depth, and pressure of your exploration. It's important to remember that the massage is meant to nurture and relax the yoni. With the palm facing up and the middle finger still inside, make a come hither motion and find the spongy area of her g-spot. This is just beneath the venus mound, behind the crown jewel, and is another part of the clitoris as a whole. This is known as the sacred spot.

The woman may feel the urge to urinate, feel some discomfort, or feel a little pleasure. Vary your speed, pressure, and pattern of movement. Move from side to side, in circles, or back and forth. It's also okay to slowly insert the finger between the pinky and middle finger in, too.

Most women won't have a problem and will enjoy the increased stimulation that comes from two fingers. Be gentle and take your time. You might want to use the thumb of the right hand to stimulate the clitoris at the same time, too. An option to attempt, if the receiver agrees, is to insert the pinky of the right hand into the anus. This is known as holding one of the mysteries of the universe. *LOL*

It's also okay to use the left hand to massage the abdomen, breasts, or clitoris at the same time. If massaging the clitoris, it's better to use an up and down motion with the rest of the hand resting on the mound. The dual stimulation of the right and left hands is going to provide a lot of pleasure for the woman. Continue to massage, using different speeds, motions, and pressure, and continue to breathe deeply and look into each other's eyes. The woman may have some powerful emotions and she may even cry. Keep breathing and continue to be gentle. Some women who have been abused sexually need this time to heal. A giving, patient, and loving partner is of great value to her. IF she has an orgasm, make sure she keeps breathing and continue to massage if she asks for it. More orgasms can occur and they may gain in intensity, and this is known as riding the wave in Tantra.

At the end of the massage, gently, slowly, and with respect remove the hands from the yoni. Allow the woman to breathe and relax in the afterglow of the massage. Holding and cuddling are great ways to prolong the satisfaction.

It is imperative that the man *not* ask for pleasure in return. This will spoil the entire moment for the receiver and she will not be as inclined to allow the yoni and the crown jewel massage to happen again. Remember, giving the massage is all about that, just giving and not expecting pleasure in return, other than the pleasure gained from giving.

Lingam Massage

The lingam is the man's genitals. It includes his penis, as well as his testes. Giving a lingam massage is a very intimate gesture from the giver and requires a lot of trust between partners.

To begin the lingam massage, have the man lie down on his back with a pillow under his head so he's able to look up at the giver. Place a pillow with a towel over it under his hips. His legs should be spread apart with his knees slightly bent. Pillows can also go under the knees, too. His genitals should be clearly visible to the giver. Before the body is contacted, deep, relaxing, breathing exercises should commence to get both partners relaxed. Gently massage the abdomen, legs, thighs, nipples, chest, and arms. Remind the receiver to breathe deeply and sink into the relaxation.

Pour a bit of oil onto the shaft of the penis and testicles. The giver should begin by gently massaging the testicles and taking care not to cause pain by applying too much pressure to this very sensitive area. The giver should massage the scrotum very gently, causing it to relax. Then the giver should massage the area above the lingam, the pubic bone. Massage the perineum, or the spot between the anus and testicles. Take some time when massaging the shaft of the penis. The speed and pressure should be varied. The giver should gently squeeze the penis at the base with the right hand, pull up and slide off the lingam, and alternate with the left hand. Take some time in repeating this process slowly and gently. Then change the direction and squeeze from the head of the penis down to the base and off. Alternate between the right and left hands.

The head of the penis should be massage as if the giver were using a juicer. Rubbing all around the tip of the penis and the shaft. In Tantra, many nerve endings exist on the lingam that will correspond with other parts of the body. It's believed that there are many ailments that can be cured with an excellent lingam massage. The lingam does not have to be hard in order for this massage to be performed! Don't worry if the lingam doesn't get hard again during the process. It will most likely get hard, go soft, and get hard again which is a great tantric experience. It's like riding the wave for women. Hardness and softness are the two ends of the pleasure spectrum, so don't be alarmed.

If the receiver appears that he may ejaculate, then the giver should back off and allow the lingam to soften a bit before the massage is resumed. Do this a few times, allowing the man come to close to ejaculation, and then backing off. It's important to remember that the goal is not to ultimately orgasm. Men can learn how to control their ejaculation through the backing off of stimulation. When they breathe deeply, it will soften their urge to ejaculate. Eventually, this mastery will allow the man to make love as long as he wishes and he can become multi-orgasmic without actually ejaculating. Orgasm and ejaculation are actually two different responses that the man is able to learn to separate. The result is an expanded sex life.

The Sacred Spot

While massaging the lingam, the giver should look for the male sacred spot. This is a small indentation about the size of a pea about midway between his anus and testicles. The giver should be gentle and push inward slowly. The man will feel this deep inside of him and he may be a bit uncomfortable at first. Eventually, this area can be worked on and softened. And he will be able to expand his orgasms and master his ejaculatory control. The lingam can be massaged with the right hand while the sacred spot is massaged with the left hand.

The giver should try to push on this spot when the man is nearing ejaculation. He may have strong emotions come up while the sacred spot is being pushed. Be the friend and the healer he needs at that moment. The giver is creating a place of intimacy and trust with the receiver.

To end the massage, when the man feels complete, gently remove the hands and cover the man's to keep him warm. Most importantly, allow him to rest for five to ten minutes quietly.

Anal Massage for Men

Some men are open to receiving an anal massage from their partner. No matter what method is used in order to massage the prostate, it cannot be touched directly. The nearest indirect access to this area is through the rectal wall, which means that there is a membrane in the way. Despite that restriction, the lobes of the prostate are very sensitive to pressure. Many sensations can be brought about through massaging this area, such as ejaculation.

The prostate is known as the hidden penis because over a third of the penis is actually buried inside the body. It's the base of the penis that can be pressed that may be similar to massaging the prostate. The effect of stimulating these three areas can be amazing for a man, as long as it's done at the same time as genital stimulation. The psychological aspects of massaging the prostate are great because of the unaccustomed nature of the penetration the man is receiving.

To prepare for this very intimate and powerful act, the receiver should be sure to be meticulously clean. The giver should have latex gloves available, not the loose ones either. It's good for a number of reasons to use gloves. The benefit of protecting the delicate anal membrane from sharp fingernails and touch skin is one, and a well-lubricated, rubber surface is going to glide in more easily than exposed skin. Lubrication should always be water based in this situation.

There are two different positions that the receiver and giver can take. Let's explore them in more detail.

Face to Face

After the receiver is completely undressed, they should assume a seated position with their back against some large pillows, around a forty-five-degree angle. He should pull his knees up to his chest but angled a bit outward. The resulting positions should be comfortable for the man and allow the giver an unobstructed view of the anus and genitals of the receiver. The giver can sit cross-legged or kneel in front of the receiver.

In order to relax the receiver, the giver can begin to massage the lower extremities, especially the abdomen. The receiver can choose to relax and close his eyes, but as the massage moves forward, he should open his eyes and maintain contact with the giver.

It's up to the giver to decide if the receiver is fully relaxed and aroused. This is when the giver should gently slip on a glove and begin lubricating the receiver's anus. This process will be lengthy and ceremonial. Begin with some circular motions and stroke the anal opening. The goal is to relax and pleasure the nervous anal opening.

The giver should *never* poke the anus with the tip of the finger, but firmly and gently add pressure with the pad of the finger. Continue to add lubrication because there can never be too much. When the anus is ready, it will allow the finger to enter. All that's need is some time and patience.

When the moment comes, the giver will notice that the finger seems to be drawn into the anus. Once it's been allowed to enter, it's best to allow the anal sphincters to become adjusted to the intrusion. It's not a good idea for the giver to move their finger in and out of the anus. There should be only one reason to remove the finger, and that's to add more lubrication.

Now the giver is ready to find the prostate. This is easily found by crooking the finger upward and feeling for an oblong, round protrusion around two inches inside the anus. Applying pressure to this prostate area will provide a variety of sensation for the receiver, and the most pleasurable one is the feeling of impending ejaculation. The application of more or less pressure on this gland will help the giver control these sensations, even to the brink of inhibiting the receiver from ejaculating. The ability to control the ejaculation through a prostate massage allows for an almost unending stimulation of the receiver's genitals. The penis can be massaged by the giver or the receiver to the point of almost ejaculating, only to be kept on the brink by lessening pressure on the prostate.

During this ebb and flow of arousal, the giver can begin to rhythmically move and insert the finger partially in and out in order to stimulate the nerve endings around the anus.

Eye contact is desirable at this stage of the massage, which allows for a few scenarios to happen.

- The giver allows the receiver to masturbate and achieve ejaculation. The giver will encourage the receiver verbally to the moment of their climax.

- The giver can masturbate the receiver's penis with their left hand as they massage the anal opening or prostate with their right hand. They should communicate intently so the receiver can obtain the most pleasure.

- The receiver might even want the giver to milk the prostate without stimulating the penis directly. To achieve this, the giver gently strokes the lobes, resulting in a gentle voiding of the prostate via the rigid or soft penis.

Facing Away

The receiver will knee with their knees apart and their behind elevated into the air while his elbows rest on a firm surface. This should be a comfortable and stable position for him.

The giver will then kneel or sit behind the receiver in a spread-legged position and have easy access and view of the anus. The giver can then position themselves to reach between the man's legs and stimulate the genitals.

The directions are the same as with face to face stimulation from this point on.

Cunnilingus

Cunnilingus is performing oral sex on a woman.

There are many women who now prefer oral sex not be performed on them, and for good reason. When it comes to having an excellent oral sex partner for a woman, he or she can be hard to find. The truth is many men obtain their information from the porn industry, and this is a gross misrepresentation of what women actually prefer when they are receiving oral pleasure.

Another reason women do not like to receive oral pleasure is because they believe their genitalia is ugly, smelly, or just not attractive, and they think their partners are not enjoying it. Unless any of this is actually true, then her partner has to tell her how much he or she enjoys giving oral to her! Reassure her that she tastes delicious, that she's beautiful down there and show her just how much it turns you on to give her oral.

Once it's established that she's willing to try it again, the first step is putting her at ease.

Men need to realize that they are not going to change a woman's relationship with her body in just one session, but he can make an effort to make her feel at ease. Instead of thinking of oral pleasure as foreplay, think of it as the main act. Many women actually enjoy oral sex more than they enjoy intercourse, but men tend to be too quick about it and don't really get her excited at all. Let her know that this is meant to bring her to climax and that it's all about her pleasure this time.

Warming Up

Now that she's satisfied that this is going to be a pleasurable experience for her, you'll then need to begin, but don't immediately press down on the clitoris! This is a huge mistake many men make, and the reason is that the woman's clitoris can be painful when it's stimulated without being aroused first. Taking your time is going to make her feel more excited and relaxed.

Spend a lot of time hugging, kissing, touching, and finding out what she wants to be stimulated during this exercise. Once the woman is aroused without the man having touched her clitoris, he should then begin to kiss his way down to between her legs.

Keep in mind that it takes most women twenty minutes to reach their first orgasm, so the man is in for the long haul. He should be comfortable with his body stretched out, his neck at a comfortable angle, and maybe a pillow beneath the woman's behind to elevate her to the proper level. If the man is not comfortable on his stomach, he can kneel at the foot of the bed with a pillow under his knees and her behind on the edge of the bed.

Find a Routine

Women prefer it when men take it easy. In fact, most of them are turned off when a man violently goes at her with his tongue. It's not a pleasurable feeling. Think of the tongue as more like a painter's brush gently stroking the canvas, up and down and side to side. Don't just focus on the clitoris, but also use the tongue on other areas of the vagina. The tongue should not be rock hard, but instead gentle and warm.

A basic routine a man can start with is to spread the woman's labia and begin by licking the area of the labia top, just above the clitoris. Use an index finger on the right hand to intersperse some finger strokes across the clitoris with some vertical tongue strokes. Remember to keep it slow.

As she becomes more aroused, insert a single or maybe two fingers into her vagina. Use the tongue to enhance arousal and then complement that arousal with the fingers. Do not try to push the tongue in and out of the vagina or move the fingers in and out of the vagina in a thrusting motion. Press the fingers upward to find the g-spot instead and apply some persistent, gentle licks to the clitoris.

With a free hand, touch her breasts and gently squeeze the nipples. Caress the stomach and cup the behind.

Remember that every woman is different. Some will prefer the clitoris be stimulated with some stroking motions while others will prefer a suckling sensation. Listen to the woman's reactions and see what works best for her. Ask her if she's not responsive, and try to be patient with her. Remember that she's most likely had some bad experiences in the past.

Pay Attention to the Commissure

The commissure is the spot above the clitoral hood and clitoris. It's a very smooth area of skin that is usually ignored by givers because it is so close to the infamous clitoris. In order to stimulate the commissure instead of the clitoris, the man should make his mouth into almost an Elvis Presley face, and then press his gum into her front commissure. Then he should make a seal between his gum and her commissure, and then perform some gentle licks to that area.

The commissure actually is connected to the clitoris beneath the skin, and so it provides some indirect stimulation to the clitoris. Remember the clitoris should not be directly stimulated until just before orgasm.

Prepare for the Orgasm

While tantric massage is not about achieving orgasm, women are going to be more likely to want this type performed more often if they do. If the woman begins to get close to orgasm, the man should pull her legs closer together in order to stimulate her more. However, there is one very important thing he should remember.

Never change the pace! Do not allow the tongue to speed up or increase in intensity despite the woman's increase in arousal and orgasm. Women like deliberate and methodical strokes rather than quick and flitting ones. They have found the pace they enjoy, and by changing it, the man will break her arousal and he has to begin again.

Once cunnilingus has been performed successfully, the man should give the woman five to ten minutes of rest between either another session or intercourse because she is currently very sensitive.

Now that you both know how to arouse each other before the actual act of intercourse, and guys remember that it takes twenty minutes for women to become fully aroused, now is the time to explore the different positions!

Chapter 9:
Tantric Sex Positions for Beginners

This is most likely what you've been waiting for, so without further ado, here are the sex positions for tantric sex. Now, keep in mind that any sex position can be turned into tantric sex by taking it slow and listening to your partner.

The Hot Seat

The man should kneel behind the woman and lean slightly backward. Then the woman kneels in front of the man with her legs between his. Their bodies should be squeezed together tightly. Have the man wrap his arms around the woman's waist and put her hands wherever he would like. Once he's inside, have the woman move up and down or move her hips in a circular motion in tandem. Take breaks when one or both partners gets too worked up or tired.

Get Down On It

Have the man sit down on the floor or on the bed in the traditional lotus position. His legs should be crossed and his heels should be on the opposite knee. The woman should face him, sitting on his lap and mounting him with her legs wrapped around his waist tightly. The couple should embrace each other and lock lips with shared breath, so that when the woman exhales, the man inhales and vice versa. As the two breathe in, the woman should rock her pelvis back and tighten her vaginal muscles. As she exhales, she should rock her pelvis forward and release her muscles. The man should mirror the woman's movements.

The Butterfly

The key is to get into the perfect position for lining up the pelvises. First, the woman should find a place she can lie down so that when the man stands in front of her, his pelvis is a foot higher than hers. Then the woman lifts her legs and rests them on the man's shoulders. He helps her tilt her pelvis upward so that her back form a straight line angling toward the man, and their pelvises meet. He can use his hands on her hips or underneath her behind in order to support her while he thrusts slowly.

Row His Boat

The man slouches in a comfortable chair and keeps his legs slightly spread. The woman straddles his lap as she faces him with her knees bent and open against his chest. Her feet are braced against the seat of the chair. As the man grips her hips, thighs, or behind, she clutches the back of the chair and moves up and down on him.

The Wow Him Powwow

The man sits down with his legs crossed and the woman straddles his legs and lowers herself onto his lap without him penetrating her. She wraps her legs around either side of him so that she's hugging his behind. Then, both partners hold each other's arms or lower back tightly and the man enters her. Both partners should rock back and forth slowly and increase their speed when desired.

The Mermaid

The woman lies face up on the edge of a bed, countertop, or desk and places a pillow underneath her behind to get a little elevation. She extends her legs straight up and keeps them close together. She then puts her hands under the pillow to raise her pelvis a little higher or uses them to hold onto the counter or desk for leverage, or can even keep them free. The man enters her as he's standing up or kneeling on the floor. He grips the woman's feet for leverage and allows him to thrust deeper.

The Sofa Spread Eagle

The woman stands on the edge of a couch or bed with her legs spread wide open. The man stands on the floor facing her and she adjusts the width of her stance so that he can easily slide between them. Their pelvises should meet and they should rock their bodies gently together.

Torrid Tidal Wave

Have the man lie at the water's edge on a beach and keep his legs straight and together. Straddle his penis and then have the woman slowly stretch out so that she's lying on top of him with their pelvises aligned. The woman should lift her torso and rest her weight on her hands. The woman's clitoris should rub against the man's pelvic bone, creating friction. The woman should also clench her behind together so that she can feel him inside of her more intensely.

Tub Tangle

Have the man recline in a tub filled with water and have the woman straddle his lap as she's facing him. When he's inside of her, the man should sit up so that the man and woman are face-to-face. Then, the woman should wrap her legs around his back and he should so the same. Their elbows should be on each other's knees, bracing them up to chest level. The man and woman should hold onto each other tightly and sway back and forth gently. Gentle kissing of above the shoulder erogenous zones is encouraged in this position.

Lap Dance

Pad a tall-backed chair, such as a dining room chair, with some pillows and have the man sit down. The woman should straddle the man and have him penetrate her as she leans back a bit, placing her hands on his knees. The woman should extend her legs, one at a time until her ankles are resting on his corresponding shoulders. Then she should gyrate on the man's pelvis slowly.

G-Force

The woman should lie down on her back and pull her knees close to her chest. Then the man should kneel in front of her, grabbing hold of her feet with his hands. The man then penetrates the woman, thrusting forward from his hips. The woman can also put her feet on the man's chest and have him hold onto her hips. This allows deeper penetration. Be careful to go slow so as not to give the woman discomfort!

Rock a Bye Booty

Have the man lie down on his back and the woman straddles him. When the man penetrates the woman, he should lift up his torso and position himself and the woman so that they're sitting face-to-face. The woman then wraps her legs tightly around the man's behind and has him do the same to her. Then the both of them link their elbows under the other's knees and lift them up to chest level. The man and woman then cradle each other in a bear-hug fashion.

The man and woman then rock back and forth and start out slow with building rhythm. The woman squeezes her PC muscles in order to keep the man from slipping out and to arouse herself more. The man or the woman can take turns kissing each other's neck and earlobes, and kissing in order to build the tension.

Baby Got Back

The man kneels as he's sitting back on his heels, and the woman has her back to him as she's standing. She lowers herself onto his penis in a squat position with her feet on either side of the man's legs. She places her hand son her thighs for balance, and he can place his hands on her behind for some support. The woman takes him about a third of the way, teasing him a few minutes, and then going deeper slowly until she's sitting in his lap. The backs of her thighs and her behind are curving into him.

This is a position where the woman is dominant and she will be in full control of the amount and lengths between pumps she will give. In order to keep eye contact through this pose, a mirror can be set up so that both partners can see one another.

Passion Pretzel

The man and woman kneel face to face. They each put the opposite foot flat on the ground and nudge closer, joining their pelvis regions. They then lean forward with their planted feet, lunge back and forth for a slow, upright adventure. This is the ultimate equality position as both couples have their hands and arms free and are able to tantalize one another as they're rocking back and forth. The woman's clitoris is also stimulated by the grinding of her pelvis region against the man's pelvic bone.

As you can see, some of these moves are only for those who are flexible, but some of them are easily enjoyed by partners who need to get back into the swing of things!

Conclusion

As you can see, tantric sex is a tantalizing and exciting new way to enjoy sexual intercourse with your partner! The two of you get to look into each other's eyes and really experience each other's arousal rather than being focused solely on your own or on your partner. By practicing tantric sex, you are taking control of your orgasms and your sexual experience, and you're able to experiment with different positions, as well as different dominant roles between partners.

Tantric sex can really spice up your sex life and help the two of you feel closer to one another both in and out of the bedroom.

BONUS

KAMA SUTRA FOR BEGINNERS

Discover The Best Essential Kama Sutra Love Making Techniques !

R. Riley

© 2015 Copyright.

Text copyright reserved. R. Riley

The contents of this book may not be reproduced, duplicated or transmitted without direct written permission from the author

Disclaimer : all attempts have been made by the author to provide factual and accurate content. No responsibility will be taken by the author for any damages caused by misuse of the content described in this book. The content of this book has been derived from various sources. Please consult a licensed professional before attempting any techniques outlined in this book.

Table of Contents

Introduction

Despite the fact that it's been a part of life since the beginning of mankind, sexual behavior is a topic that is often perceived as a taboo subject in today's society. Yet, the more we run away from it, the more likely we are to encounter problems within our sex lives. Like any other aspect of a relationship, sexual behavior requires openness and communication in order for both parties to be continually satisfied. There's no better way to establish a healthy, satisfying intimate relationship than studying the Kama Sutra.

Anyone who is unfamiliar with the Kama Sutra may be surprised to know that it's actually an ancient text that was developed thousands of years ago. Specifically, it's believed that the Kama Sutra was written anywhere from 400 BCE to 200 CE. It was originally composed in Sanskrit by the Hindu philosopher Vātsyāyana.

Though the Kama Sutra is often regarded as a "sex manual," it is in fact much more about embracing the pleasures of life than about achieving specific sexual positions. In fact, the word "kama" refers to desire, while "sutra" refers to rules, or the thread that ties all things together. The pursuit of pleasures is known as one of the four aims of life within Hindu traditions. In other words, the Kama Sutra was written as a formula for achieving one's desires.

It is said that the writer of the Kama Sutra, Vātsyāyana, did not believe that sex should be regarded as an off-limits, "bad" behavior; although, he did express the notion that performing sexual acts in a detached, unemotional manner should be considered sinful.

Although the text is ancient by today's standards, the principles found within it are by no means outdated. In fact, it's possible that just about any romantic relationship could benefit by including some of the Kama Sutra ideologies within its sexual endeavors.

Throughout this eBook, we'll explore the ways in which you can implement Kama Sutra practices in your love life to connect on a deeper level with your significant others. Everything from kissing to sexual intercourse can be enhanced so that you can create a more loving, intimate relationship and experience a greater sense of pleasure. You and your loved one can follow along and go at your own pace, exploring the notion of the Kama Sutra in a way that works best for your relationship.

Chapter 1:
Kissing

When kissing comes to mind, one might imagine that the act of locking lips should be pretty straightforward. After all, kissing has been regarded as a symbol of love, seemingly since the beginning of mankind. It's typically the first indication that a relationship is progressing to a more romantic level, and when done properly, it should send both parties into a state of passion, desire, and excitement.

What do we mean by "properly?" Again, you may think that as long as you've done it enough times, you know all there is to know about the act of kissing. Unless you're an expert on the Kama Sutra, though, that most likely isn't true. Here's why: within the Kama Sutra, there are multiple different ways to kiss your lover, including the pressed kiss, the straight kiss, and the turned kiss.

Oftentimes, we fall into specific patterns when it comes to our love lives, either because we've become comfortable in our routines or because we're hesitant to try new things. This happens quite often in relationships that have been ongoing for at least a few years, but it doesn't have to be that way. If you and your loved one are interested in exploring different techniques, you shouldn't hold back. Kissing should not be done complacently - like other aspects of physical touch, it's important to try to express your emotions and passions through the delivery of your kiss. Likewise, you should be the recipient of passion when you are kissed back.

In addition to acting as a gateway to further romantic physical activity within a relationship, kissing is also an essential element of foreplay. In other words, kissing should, in some way, take place before you and your partner engage in lovemaking, regardless of how long you've been together or how rushed the act may be. Oftentimes, outside factors get in the way of a couple's love lives; jobs, families, and other stressors can make it difficult to find the time or peace of mind for sex. Yet, a couple shouldn't rely on simply going through the motions each time they engage in sexual activity. Instead, they should bring passion into the mix each time they make love. One way to ensure that is by practicing Kama Sutra kissing techniques.

Perhaps the most common kissing technique is the bent kiss. In order to achieve this type of kiss, each party bends his or her head towards the other. The kissing takes place as the heads are bent at an angle.

The straight kiss is another common kissing technique. The Kama Sutra describes it as a kiss in which both lovers' lips are brought directly towards one another. This kiss works for some couples better than it does for others. Just be sure to avoid injuring your noses if you use this kissing method.

The turned kiss is considered to be a bit more passionate. In this technique, one person turns his or her head up to face the other individual, and the other individual typically will hold the head of that person. The added touch of the chin can be very sensual and can add an element of lust to an ordinary kiss. If you'd like to try out the turned kiss and you're the taller person in your relationship, place your hand gently under the chin of your loved one to tilt his or her head up, and then bestow a kiss. If you would like to be the recipient of the turned kiss or you're the shorter individual, you can encourage your partner to place his or her hand on your chin by grabbing his hand and placing it where you'd like it to be; or, you could always simply ask him or her to do it. Keep in mind that you or your partner's height doesn't have to be the determining factor for engaging in this type of kiss - one of you could always sit while the other stands.

Another passionate method of Kama Sutra kissing is the pressed kiss. In this variation, one person presses the other individual's lower lip with great force, using both of his or her lips. To try this on your lover, pucker his or her bottom lip out slightly using your index finger immediately prior to your kiss.

Keep in mind that any of these kissing variations can lead to tongue kissing. Referred to in the Kama Sutra as "the fighting for the tongue," this form of kissing takes place when either party's tongue touches the other individual's teeth, palate, or tongue. Typically, this type of open-mouthed kissing has the potential to lead to further sexual activity.

Most importantly, make sure to always include kissing in your sexual repertoire. Overlooking the act of kissing can make a lovemaking experience dull and disconnected. Feel free to experiment with the techniques listed above for unique and new approaches to kissing that will kick start your sexual experience with your loved one.

45404031R00051

Made in the USA
San Bernardino, CA
07 February 2017